VPS TOOLKIT
Ubuntu Server LTS 2014 Edition

VPS TOOLKIT
Ubuntu Server LTS 2014 Edition

edited by:

Davide Gatti

DeeWHY

2014

First Printing: 2014

ISBN 978-1-326-07799-0

DeeWHY
London, United Kingdom

www.deewhy.org

Ordering:
Special discounts are available on quantity purchases by corporations, associations, educators, and others. For details, contact the publisher at the above listed address.

        http://deewhy.org/contacts/

e-mail   buy@deewhy.org

Dedication

Ciao amico mio.

Sempre sul cuore.

Summary

Forewords

This guide is intended for webmasters who wish to overcome the limitations of traditional hosting space. The use of a Virtual Private Server allows to increase productivity in terms of time, total control of the filesystem and often let lower management costs. The VPS also allows to use all those applications which require server-side rooting control.

Particular attention will be dealt with the part relating to security, developing the critical settings at the same time in every steps of the server configuration.

All the arguments will be treated with examples and commands using Linux Ubuntu Server 14.04.1 LTS, but from the logical point of view the concepts may be completely withheld in any recent Linux Server OS in a simple and fast way.

Introduction

What's a VPS ?

A Virtual Private Server is Virtual Machine that permit to get over the classic commercial hosting space because it allows full control of on the server side - it's often used for development and testing purposing too.

When a pure VPS is ready to be accessed online after the purchase from the service-provider or after a freshly re-installation, it comes with some features and basically IP address to be reached to connect it on, so as a minimum we should have:

- Root access credentials;
- IPv4 address and sometime IPv6 address / VPS Host Name;

plus some kind of Online Keyboard Replication to simulate the fact the user is virtually directly present onto the remote machine; that could be done throw a KVM server for keyboard remote simulation or a Remote Control Server i.e. RealVNC, TeamViewer or other in case of a GUI interface is installed (not so often on a VPS).

VPS TOOLKIT

:: 1 :: Preliminary Steps

Remote connection to the new VPS

So let's connect to the VPS with an SSH Client. In a Windows OS environment in most cases is necessary to download the SSH Client form the external i.e. PuTTY, using LINUX – MacOSX just run the Terminal and run the command 'ssh' with the appropriate options. The standard port to connect throw is the number 22, we can use the VPS IP address for now but if there's a DNS Server somewhere that can resolve the VPS Host Name (and there's it in almost all cases) or if we've already imposed the right redirection for a domain name, it's possible to use that as well.

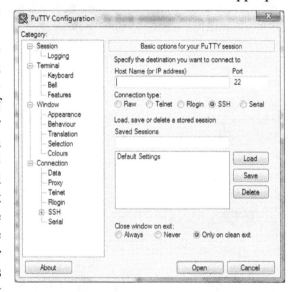

Let's consider this environment:
OS: UBUNTU server 14.04.01 - Public VPS IP address: 192.168.1.11
UserID: root - UserPSW: x6-tr8-fx9

from the Terminal:

ssh 192.168.1.11 or *ssh 192.168.1.11 –l root* (to directly put the UserID / fit the same using PuTTY for Windows)

> *:: pay attention to the fact, when prompting the password nothing will be showed for security reasons ::*

Starting the VPS configuration - Preliminary steps

The first thing to do when accessing a new VPS is check the network configuration, to do it type:

ifconfig

and annotate in particular what network adapters are configured and associated to the public IP addresses. Then make the OS up to date:

apt-get update && apt-get upgrade

confirming 'Yes' :: literally, case sensitive :: when asked to proceed.
On a new server, there are a few configuration steps that you should take early on as part of the basic setup. This will increase the security, usability and will gives a solid foundation for subsequent actions.

Root Login: clarifications
To log into the server initially, you will need to know your server's public IP address and the password for the "root" user's account.
The root user is the administrative user in a Linux environment that has very broad privileges. Because of the heightened privileges of the root account, you are actually discouraged from using it on a

4

regular basis. This is because part of the power inherent with the root account is the ability to make very destructive changes, even by accident.

Now, we'll set up an alternative user account with a reduced scope of influence for day-to-day work. You'll learn how to gain increased privileges during the times when you need them.

The first step is to log into the server, and the only account we start out with is the root account. We can connect to the server by using the ssh command in the terminal.

You will most likely see a warning in your terminal window that looks like this:

The authenticity of host '123.123.123.123 (123.123.123.123)' can't be established.
ECDSA key fingerpring is
79:95:46:1a:ab:37:11:8e:86:54:36:38:bb:3c:fa:c0.
Are you sure you want to continue connecting (Yes/No)?

Here, your computer is basically telling you that it doesn't recognize your remote server. Since this is your first time connecting, this is completely expected.

Go ahead and type "Yes" to accept the connection. Afterwards, you'll need to enter the password for the root account.

Change Password
You are not likely to remember the password that is currently set for your root account. You can change the password to something you will remember more easily by typing:

passwd

It will ask you to enter and confirm your new password. During this process, you will not see anything show up on your screen as you type. This is intentional and is there so that people looking over your shoulder cannot guess your password by the number of characters.

Create a New User
At this point, we're prepared to add the new user account that we will use to log in from now on; select whatever name you'd like:

adduser demo

You will be asked a few questions, starting with the account password. Fill out the password and, optionally, fill in any of the additional information if you would like. This is not required and you can just hit "ENTER" in any field you wish to skip.

Root Privileges
Now, we have a new user account with regular account privileges. However, we may sometimes need to do administrative tasks.
To avoid having to log out of our normal user and log back in as the root account, we can set up what is known as "*sudo*" privileges for our normal account. This will allow our normal user to run commands with administrative privileges by putting the word "*sudo*" before each command.
To add these privileges to our new account, we need to use a command called *visudo*. This will open a configuration file:

visudo

Scroll down until you find a section that deals with user privileges. It will look similar to this:

 # User privilege specification
root   ALL=(ALL:ALL) ALL

While this might look complicated, we don't need to worry about that. All we need to do is add another line below it that follows the format, replacing "demo" with the user you created:

 # User privilege specification
root   ALL=(ALL:ALL) ALL
demo   ALL=(ALL:ALL) ALL

After this is done, press CTRL-X to exit. You will have to type "Y" to save the file and then press "ENTER" to confirm the file location.

Configure SSH (Optional)
Now that we have our new account, we can secure our server a little bit by modifying the configuration of SSH (the program that allows us to log in remotely).
Begin by opening the configuration file with your text editor as root:

nano /etc/ssh/sshd_config

:: Change SSH Port
The first option is to change the port that SSH runs on. Find the line that looks like this:

Port 22

If we change this number to something in between 1025 and 65536, the SSH service on our server will look for connections on a different port. This is sometimes helpful because unauthorized users sometimes try to break into servers by attacking SSH. If you change the location, they will need to complete the extra step of sniffing it out.

If you change this value, you will need to keep in mind that your server is running on the new port. For this example, it is changed to 4444 as a demonstration. This means that when connecting is necessary to tell the SSH client to use this new, non-default port. We'll get to that later. For now, modify that value to the selection:

Port 4444

:: Restrict Root Login
Next, we need to find the line that looks like this:

PermitRootLogin yes

Here, we have the option to disable root logins through SSH. This is generally a more secure setting since we can now access our server through our normal user account and escalate privileges when necessary.
You can modify this line to "no" if you want to disable root logins:

PermitRootLogin no

:: Explicitly Permit Certain Users
You can go one step further and specify the exact users that you wish to be able to log into your server. Any user not on the list you configure will not be permitted to log in through SSH.
Be careful when configuring this option, as you can easily lock yourself out if you mistype your username.
For this option, you'll have to add the line yourself. You should use the following syntax. Remember to replace *"demo"* with the username that you configured:

AllowUsers demo

When you are finished making any of the optional changes above, save and close the file using the method we went over earlier (CTRL-X, then "Y", then "ENTER").

Reload SSH
Now that we have made our changes, we need to restart the SSH service so that it will use our new configuration.
Type this to restart SSH:

service ssh restart

Now, before we log out of the server, we should test our new configuration. We do not want to disconnect until we can confirm that new connections can be established successfully.
Open a new terminal window. In the new window, we need to begin a new connection to our server. This time, instead of using the root account, we want to use the new account that we created.
If you changed the port number that SSH is running on, you'll need to tell your client about the new port as well. You can do this by using the *-p 4444* syntax, where "4444" is the port you configured. Substitute your own information where it is appropriate:

ssh -p 4444 demo@server_ip_address

You will be prompted for the new user's password that you configured. After that, you will be logged in as your new user.
Remember, if you need to run a command with root privileges, type "*sudo*" before it like this:

sudo [command_to_run]

To terminate and exit the ssh sessions, type:

exit   or   *logout*

9

WEBMIN

Webmin is a web-based interface for system administration for Unix and its derivates (e.g. Linux). Using the DEB version of Webmin, first download the file from the downloads page running the commands:

wget http://prdownloads.sourceforge.net/webadmin/webmin_1.710_all.deb

(at the time of this book the release V1.710 was the latest stable); then run the deb package

dpkg --install webmin_1.710_all.deb

that will install it automatically to */usr/share/webmin*, the administration username set to '*root*' and the password to the current root password 'x6-tr8-fx9' (considering the last example environment).
Should now be possible accessing remotely and login to Webmin to the URL http://192.168.1.11:10000/ with internet browser
In most cases, especially with new installed systems, the OS complains about missing dependencies, so you can install them with the command:

apt-get install perl libnet-ssleay-perl openssl libauthen-pam-perl libpam-runtime libio-pty-perl apt-show-versions python

or just doing it automatically with the command:

apt-get install –f

now let's pass to the internet browser - the Terminal window can stay opened.

After logged in the webmin's main page shows the *System Information* summary; first of first let's secure the connection; so now click on Webmin (right up side), then open up Webmin Configuration, select the SSL Encryption icon, then select the first task SSL setting and flag *Yes* on *Enable SSL if available?*;

now just reload Webmin (e.g. press F5 on Windows or CTRL+R on MacOS X) and login again after skipping/accepting the certificate notification. Here's again the main System Information page but the protocol is not http anymore but it is now '*https*' - the red line on 'https' means the certificate is not provided by an accredited Certificate Authority - its details can be viewed on the Current Certificate's task over SSL Encryption, it is possible to install and use an accredited certificate but that's not really useful at this stage (https, written in green).

VPS TOOLKIT

:: 2 :: Server Configuration

Host & Name

Let's go back to the Terminal. To assign a personalized name/hostname to the system – choose a text editor for the console, here 'nano' – eventually *apt-get install nano*; then type:

hostname –f and observe the output;

so now it's the moment to assign a Domain Name to the system (just in case) or rather go to the website of the hosting provider, access their panel and configure a new 'A Record' aiming it to the public IPv4 address of the VPS server, as well as a new 'AAAA' record for the IPv6 if available. So, consider the updated environment:

Let's consider this environment:
OS: UBUNTU server 14.04.01 - Public VPS IP address: 192.168.1.11
UserID: root - UserPSW: x6-tr8-fx9
FQN Domain: example.com

to assign 'example.com' as host-name, edit the *hostname* & the *hosts* file:

nano /etc/hostname
        :: writing at the very beginning of the file *example*

and then

13

nano /etc/hosts
:: adding a line in the IPv4 section of the file, as following:

192.168.1.11   example.com example
insert [IPv6]   example.com example (just in case)

:: nano (ctlr+o to save, ctrl+x to exit back to the Terminal)

to ensure the changes taking place the network interface service must be restarted. Despite it's possible to do this prompting:

/etc/init.d/network restart or *service networking restart*

just really go back to the internet browser where we left Webmin opened. Then, main page, System Information, click on the current System hostname and IP address (then return to the network configuration) and confirm by clicking Apply Configuration.

Take some time to observe the network configuration on Webmin, remembering what noted at the beginning with the command *ifconfig*. Also consider now it's the moment to start to appreciate the fact it's really possible to quick swap between Webmin and the Terminal to speed up every kind of configuration; as well, that's a very good way to perform fast double-check of every setup before, while and after setting up the system.

Tip:
try now to reboot the system and take a note of the time it will require to complete this action, because now there're quite not daemon / software servers running on it if not those from the original configuration as when it was freshly installed. To do this:

Log out from ssh: *logout*

Type the VPS's Public IP address:

ping 192.168.1.11 or *ping example.com*

:: Terminal outside ssh

Linux, MacOS, etc. stay on the Terminal – Windows run *cmd.exe* and use the ping command with the '-t' option, so typing:

ping 192.168.1.11 -t or *ping example.com –t*

After this, go back to Webmin, then System, Boot and Shutdown , click and click again to confirm on Reboot System. Observe the running *ping* command and chronometer the time the system is down. A good average time for a standard VPS to complete a rebooting should be around or less 30 seconds. Annotate the rebooting time of the VPS now.

```
64 bytes from 192.168.1.11: icmp_seq=3 ttl=64 time=3.561 ms
64 bytes from 192.168.1.11: icmp_seq=4 ttl=64 time=3.417 ms
64 bytes from 192.168.1.11: icmp_seq=5 ttl=64 time=3.614 ms
64 bytes from 192.168.1.11: icmp_seq=6 ttl=64 time=3.476 ms
64 bytes from 192.168.1.11: icmp_seq=7 ttl=64 time=1.738 ms
Request timeout for icmp_seq 8
Request timeout for icmp_seq 9
Request timeout for icmp_seq 10
Request timeout for icmp_seq 11
Request timeout for icmp_seq 12
Request timeout for icmp_seq 13
Request timeout for icmp_seq 14
Request timeout for icmp_seq 15
Request timeout for icmp_seq 16
Request timeout for icmp_seq 17
Request timeout for icmp_seq 18
Request timeout for icmp_seq 19
Request timeout for icmp_seq 20
Request timeout for icmp_seq 21
Request timeout for icmp_seq 22
Request timeout for icmp_seq 23
Request timeout for icmp_seq 24
Request timeout for icmp_seq 25
Request timeout for icmp_seq 26
Request timeout for icmp_seq 27
Request timeout for icmp_seq 28
Request timeout for icmp_seq 29
Request timeout for icmp_seq 30
Request timeout for icmp_seq 31
Request timeout for icmp_seq 32
Request timeout for icmp_seq 33
Request timeout for icmp_seq 34
Request timeout for icmp_seq 35
Request timeout for icmp_seq 36
Request timeout for icmp_seq 37
Request timeout for icmp_seq 38
Request timeout for icmp_seq 39
Request timeout for icmp_seq 40
Request timeout for icmp_seq 41
Request timeout for icmp_seq 42
Request timeout for icmp_seq 43
Request timeout for icmp_seq 44
Request timeout for icmp_seq 45
Request timeout for icmp_seq 46
64 bytes from 192.168.1.11: icmp_seq=46 ttl=64 time=1030.471 ms
64 bytes from 192.168.1.11: icmp_seq=47 ttl=64 time=25.288 ms
64 bytes from 192.168.1.11: icmp_seq=48 ttl=64 time=3.698 ms
```

FIREWALL

Introducing the firewall

Setting up a good firewall is an essential step to take in securing any modern operating system. Most Linux distributions are shiped with a few different firewall tools that we can use to configure our firewalls. We'll be covering the *iptables* firewall.
Iptables is a standard firewall included in most Linux distributions by default (a modern variant called *nftables* will begin to replace it). It is actually a front end to the kernel-level net filter hooks that can manipulate the Linux network stack. It works by matching each packet that crosses the networking interface against a set of rules to decide what to do.

How iptables Works
Before we get started discussing the actual commands needed to control iptables and build a firewall policy, let's go over some terminology and discuss how iptables works.

The iptables firewall operates by comparing network traffic against a set of rules. The rules define the characteristics that a packet must have to match the rule, and the action that should be taken for matching packets.
There are many options to establish which packets match a specific rule. You can match the packet protocol type, the source or destination address or port, the interface that is being used, its relation to previous packets, etc.
When the defined pattern matches, the action that takes place is called a target. A target can be a final policy decision for the packet, such as accept, or drop. It can also be move the packet to a different chain for processing, or simply log the encounter. There are many options.

These rules are organized into groups called chains. A chain is a set of rules that a packet is checked against sequentially. When the packet matches one of the rules, it executes the associated action and is not checked against the remaining rules in the chain.

A user can create chains as needed. There are three chains defined by default. They are:

- INPUT: This chain handles all packets that are addressed to your server;
- OUTPUT: This chain contains rules for traffic created by your server;
- FORWARD: This chain is used to deal with traffic destined for other servers that are not created on your server. This chain is basically a way to configure your server to route requests to other machines.

Each chain can contain zero or more rules, and has a default policy. The policy determines what happens when a packet drops through all of the rules in the chain and does not match any rule. You can either drop the packet or accept the packet if no rules match.

Through a module that can be loaded via rules, iptables can also track connections. This means you can create rules that define what happens to a packet based on its relationship to previous packets. We call this capability "state tracking", "connection tracking", or configuring the "state machine".
For our purposes, we are mainly going to be covering the configuration of the INPUT chain, since it contains the set of rules that will help us deny unwanted traffic directed at our server.

IPv4 & IPv6

The net-filter firewall that is included in the Linux kernel keeps IPv4 and IPv6 traffic completely separate. Likewise, the tools used to manipulate the tables that contain the firewall rule-sets are distinct as well. If you have IPv6 enabled on your server, you will have to configure both tables to address the traffic your server is subjected to.

The regular iptables command is used to manipulate the table containing rules that govern IPv4 traffic. For IPv6 traffic, a companion command called ip6tables is used. This is an important point to internalize, as it means that any rules that you set with iptables will have no affect on packets using version 6 of the protocol.
The syntax between these twin commands is the same, so creating a ruleset for each of these tables is not too overwhelming. Just remember to modify both tables whenever you make a change. The iptables command will make the rules that apply to IPv4 traffic, and the ip6tables command will make the rules that apply to IPv6 traffic.

You must be sure to use the appropriate IPv6 addresses of your server to craft the ip6tables rules.

Things to Keep in Mind

Now that we know how iptables directs packets that come through its interface (direct the packet to the appropriate chain, check it against each rule until one matches, issue the default policy of the chain if no match is found), we can begin to see some pitfalls to be aware of as we make rules.

First, we need to make sure that we have rules to keep current connections active if we implement a default drop policy. This is especially important if you are connected to your server through SSH. If you accidentally implement a rule or policy that drops your current connection, you can always log into your VPS by using the web console, which provides out-of-band access - every VPS is provided to a method to do this.

Another thing to keep in mind is that the order of the rules in each chain matter. A packet must not come across a more general rule that it matches if it is meant to match a more specific rule. Because of this, rules near the top of a chain should have a higher level of specificity than rules at the bottom. You should match specific cases first, and then provide more general rules to match broader patterns. If a packet falls through the entire chain (doesn't match any rules), it will hit the most general rule, the default policy.

For this reason, a chain's default policy very strongly dictates the types of rules that will be included in the chain. A chain with the default policy of ACCEPT will contain rules that explicitly drop packets. A chain that defaults to DROP will contain exceptions for packets that should be specifically accepted.

Configuration

Following the standard procedure, the way to setup a firewall for the first time on a remote server is starting to stay with the firewall down and:

1. close every access;
2. configure the needed opening, basically to permit the server's owner to reach the server from a remote location;
3. fire up the firewall;
4. open up every following access when necessary while proceeding with the configuration, only for the necessary accesses.

Let's do it. The iptables native firewall comes with a simple way to close every access, so if it were fire up without any rules in this case, it were impossible to reach the system from the external.

Access via SSH to the VPS and type:

iptables -v -L   :: the output should be:

Chain INPUT (policy ACCEPT)
target prot opt source destination

Chain FORWARD (policy ACCEPT)
target prot opt source destination

Chain OUTPUT (policy ACCEPT)
target prot opt source destination

this shows all the accesses are permitted; now type:

iptables -A INPUT -i lo -j ACCEPT
iptables -A INPUT -m state --state RELATED,ESTABLISHED -j ACCEPT
iptables -A INPUT -p icmp -j ACCEPT

iptables -A INPUT -p tcp –m tcp --dport 22 -j ACCEPT
iptables -A INPUT -p tcp –m udp --dport 22 -j ACCEPT

iptables -A INPUT -p tcp -m tcp --dport 10000 -j ACCEPT
iptables -A INPUT -p tcp -m tcp --dport 10000 -j ACCEPT

and in most cases and also considering the instance we are study-ing:

iptables -A FORWARD -j DROP
iptables -A OUTPUT -j ACCEPT

now, to change the INPUT POLICY type:

iptables -P INPUT DROP

and then, following up our instance:

iptables -P FORWARD DROP
iptables -P OUTPUT DROP

then, to verify the results type:

iptables –v –L

it is clear, if we want to permit the INPUT traffic to the web port 80 we have to add:

iptables -A INPUT -p tcp –m tcp --dport 80 -j ACCEPT

etc. etc. for any other port or service we desire to permit. To save this configuration in a file:

iptables-save > /etc/iptables-ipv4.rules

and to load it from scratch:

iptables-restore < /etc/iptables-ipv4.rules

but for now if we reboot the system we'll lost the current configuration, so to load it automatically, open the file */etc/network/interfaces*, and add a line on it:

nano */etc/network/interfaces*

        ...
    pre-up iptables-restore < /etc/iptables-ipv4.rules

save and close the file (ctrl+o / enter / ctrl+x).

Just in case we need to set up the firewall for the IPv6, basically it's possible to use the same file saved for the IPv4, but there're some little differences sometime in the syntax, as for example the ICMP (ping); the command to use is *ip6tables* instead of *iptables*, modifying a copy of the file *iptables-ipv4.rules*:

cp /etc/iptables-ipv4.rules /etc/iptables-ipv6.rules

nano /etc/ iptables-ipv6.rules

changing the line: *-A INPUT -p icmp -j ACCEPT*
to the line: *-A INPUT -p ipv6-icmp -j ACCEPT*

to load it and make the IPv6 setup taking place:

ip6tables-restore < /etc/iptables-ipv6.rules

and to finally check it out:

ip6tables –v -L

All done, now the firewall is operative. If we like to make the configuration in a GUI with Webmin for IPv4, just rename the file *iptables-ipv4.rules to iptables.up.rules* and Webmin will automatically read the current configuration, and just deal to the firewall setting by that point.

To check the firewall configuration gradually when proceeding with the configuration using Webmin, use the Terminal typing:

iptables -v –L

depending on which rules are running, the output will be something like this:

```
Chain INPUT (policy DROP 1176 packets, 175K bytes)
 pkts bytes target     prot opt in     out     source               destination
 7776 1305K ACCEPT     all  --  lo      any     anywhere             anywhere
77678   45M ACCEPT     all  --  any     any     anywhere             anywhere             state RELATED,ESTABLISHED
    0     0 ACCEPT     icmp --  any     any     anywhere             anywhere
    2   104 ACCEPT     tcp  --  any     any     anywhere             anywhere             tcp dpt:ssh
    0     0 ACCEPT     udp  --  any     any     anywhere             anywhere             udp dpt:ssh
    0     0 DROP       tcp  --  any     any     anywhere             anywhere             tcp dpt:ftp
    0     0 DROP       tcp  --  any     any     anywhere             anywhere             tcp dpt:http
   21  1344 ACCEPT     tcp  --  any     any     anywhere             anywhere             tcp dpt:webmin
    6   284 ACCEPT     tcp  --  any     any     anywhere             anywhere             tcp dpt:1723
    0     0 ACCEPT     tcp  --  any     any     anywhere             anywhere             tcp dpt:47
 1133 58400 ACCEPT     tcp  --  any     any     anywhere             anywhere             tcp dpt:http-alt
    0     0 ACCEPT     udp  --  any     any     anywhere             anywhere             udp dpt:http-alt
    0     0 ACCEPT     tcp  --  any     any     anywhere             anywhere             tcp dpt:domain
 4438  294K ACCEPT     udp  --  any     any     anywhere             anywhere             udp dpt:domain
 1744  141K ACCEPT     udp  --  any     any     anywhere             anywhere             udp dpt:netbios-ns
  437  105K ACCEPT     udp  --  any     any     anywhere             anywhere             udp dpt:netbios-dgm
   46  2560 ACCEPT     tcp  --  any     any     anywhere             anywhere             tcp dpt:netbios-ssn
   30  1896 ACCEPT     tcp  --  any     any     anywhere             anywhere             tcp dpt:microsoft-ds

Chain FORWARD (policy DROP 0 packets, 0 bytes)
 pkts bytes target     prot opt in     out     source               destination
    0     0 DROP       all  --  any     any     anywhere             anywhere

Chain OUTPUT (policy ACCEPT 0 packets, 0 bytes)
 pkts bytes target     prot opt in     out     source               destination
91319   43M ACCEPT     all  --  any     any     anywhere             anywhere
```

Users & Groups Setup

Choosing the right user-names

There's a kind of policy regarding the user-names in Linux. Trying to install a new Operating System in a general machine starting from the installation CD-Rom some user names are not allowed because are already reserved and there're also some security reasons. In general this is not true in a VPS but some rules must to be applied to better organize the work in progress.

In a web system environment is easy to imagine that 'hostmaster', 'webmaster' and 'postmaster' are common names specifically used for assigning the rights to supervise in various ways the web machine(s) and its contents, but they are generally not reserved from the OS as for instance 'root', 'administrator' and, from the practical point of view, 'www-data'; same thing for the groups and then, immediately after when choosing the right email's names. Consider the email's names often used as UserID when logging-in on plenty of applications.

The server-side comprehensive understanding of this point require to know how the most used daemons and software-servers works but again, every webmaster faced the situation several times from just the hosting-side as well. This is the first step designed to overcome the limitations of an hosting solution to a (quite) fully controlled server as a VPS.

The choice of user names and especially the path which they are associated is critical but allows to perfectly organize the works, especially in view of every future grows, applications installation and multiple domain managing.

So let's start the configuration. The purpose here's to deploy online a machine to be surfed from the public and allows the owner to fully control everyone want to reach this machine, whether inscribed or not registered inside the Operating System, giving, however, a logical collocation to handle the level of interaction.

Understand the needings
To deploy a web machine that can substitute an hosting space and be better configurable and fast to set up; starting from what a webmaster expects, there should be something like:

UserName	SSH access / OS user	ftp access	Super User rights
webmaster	yes or no / yes	yes	no
postmaster	no / no	no	no
mailmaster	no / yes or no	no	no
hostmaster	yes / yes	yes	yes

webmaster — the user with the right to upload, delete, edit and change the 'chmod' inside the web hosting space, classically via FTP; this user is included in the system group 'www-data' and control the access of the files and the directories exposed to the external internet; often he control also the databases and the databases' users;

postmaster — the user who have the rights to post new contents, moderate a forum or a blog, he only have an email assigned from the system's owner and his rights aren't assigned at Operating System's level but only inside the

25

loaded web's application e.g. phpbb, Joomla!, wordpress, etc. ... ;

mailmaster in a VPS rarely there's a complete mail server installed, because the very limited disk space, but basically just an SMTP server used for sending system's email i.e. servicing the php capability of php sendmail. Instead this user is the one who can create, delete modify the email addresses provided for example by the service provider, a proper webmail server, or an external CRM server;

hostmaster considering the system's paths where the web server aim the external internet users to show them the web pages, every domain, their virtual hosts and then the relative directories/folders are placed over the control of this user, so the directories/folders of the webmaster(s) are underneath of the hostmaster control; he's in effect a system administrator and often he has the rights to fully control the whole system like the root user; in case of multi domain panel i.e. cpanel, zpanel, etc, the hostmaster is the principal actor of the system administration.

To each user whether or not part of the Operating System are assigned e-mail addresses as for instance:

webmaster   ::   webmaster@mydomain.com

postmaster	::	postmaster@mydomain.com
mailmaster	::	mailmaster@mydomain.com
hostmaster	::	hostmaster@mydomain.com

and more, as for instance: buy@mydomain.com,
equires@mydomain.com,
info@mydomain.com,
noreply@mydomain.com, etc.

one of the first thing to be decided is which are the email addresses to be utilized for the purpose of sending emails from the machine (e.g. using phpmail); again, from the practical point of view they often can really be set up in a simple way throw the most famous web applications i.e. portal systems, forums, blogs, etc., in most cases without access the SSH and manually edit the configuration files, but via administrations web pages.

Users & Groups creation
Let's create the Web Master user; figure out, for now, a web machine with only one domain 'example.com'; here is:

Real Name:	Web Master
User Name:	webmaster
Password:	a1b2c3d4
Home Directory:	/var/www
Shell:	/bin/bash
Groups	users; www-data; ssh

Access the Terminal via ssh with the root credials and type:

mkdir /var/www

this to create a folder to use it as the webmaster's home directory; after that, leave the Terminal and access Webmin with the root credentials again, then open up System and click on Users and Groups; to create a new user:

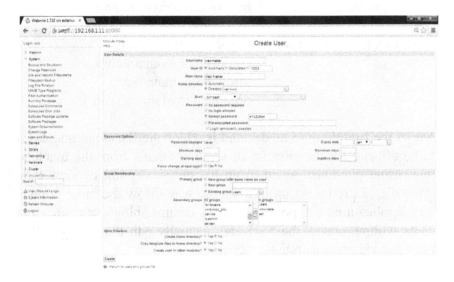

and click on Create. Now it's also the moment to restrict the access to the ssh server, or better to decide to allow it only to the ssh group. To do this on Webmin open up 'Servers', then click on 'SSH Server' and choose the icon 'Access Control':

then click on 'Only allow members of groups', choosing the group 'ssh'. This procedure must be done in general every time creating a new user, putting it inside the desired groups and assigning the desired access to the services. This will done for the first thing to the FTP server for the webmaster in particular.

:: Note, in a web-server that host just one or few domains it's a common practice to give to the webmaster the 'sudo' rights, to use it as root user; in this case remember to include the root group too.

Now back to the Terminal and type:

chown –R webmaster:www-data /var/www

this assign as owner the webmaster home directory and eventually all the files inside it to the webmaster and to the group www-data, using the recursive –R option.
Giving the SSH access to a user without touching the default ssh server configuration, everyone is permitted to access (viewing as minimum) every directory all around the server; the above procedure can partially avoid this, discriminating first who is allowed to access the ssh - but to definitely jail an user into his home directory a chrooting procedure must be implemented into the configuration; more simple but same thing for the FTP server.

SSH – Jail users into their own home directories
To the Terminal, edit the */etc/ssh/sshd_config* file with the favorite text editor:

nano /etc/ssh/sshd_config

add or modify the Subsystem sftp line to look like the following:

Subsystem sftp internal-sftp
add this block of settings to the end of the file:
Match group filetransfer
*   ChrootDirectory %h*

29

X11Forwarding no
AllowTcpForwarding no
Force Command internal-sftp

Save the changes to your file. Restart OpenSSH:

service ssh restart

OpenSSH has been successfully modified.

Modify User Accounts
Set up the correct new groups, ownership, and permissions for your user accounts; create a system group for users whom to be restrict to SFTP access:

addgroup --system filetransfer

modify the user accounts that wish to restrict to SFTP. Issue the following commands for each account, substituting the appropriate username. Please keep in mind that this will prevent these users from being able to log into a remote shell session.

usermod -G filetransfer username

chown root:root /home/username

chmod 755 /home/username

These users will now be unable to create files in their home directories, since these directories are owned by the root user.

Next, create new directories for each user, to which they will have full access. Issue the following commands for each user, changing the directories created to suit your needs:

cd /home/username

mkdir docs public_html

*chown username:filetransfer **

the users should now be able to log into their accounts via SFTP and transfer files to and from their assigned subdirectories, but they shouldn't be able to see the rest of the filesystem.

VPS TOOLKIT

:: 3 :: WebServer

APACHE Web Server Vs the rest

 The Apache HTTP Server is a Web server application notable for playing a key role in the initial growth of the World Wide Web. Originally based on the NCSA HTTPd server, development of Apache began in early 1995 after work on the NCSA code stalled. Apache quickly overtook NCSA HTTPd as the dominant HTTP server, and has remained the most popular HTTP server in use since April 1996. In 2009, it became the first Web server software to serve more than 100 million Web sites.

Apache is developed and maintained by an open community of developers under the auspices of the Apache Software Foundation. Most commonly used on a Unix-like system, the software is available for a wide variety of operating systems, including-
ing Unix, FreeBSD, Linux, Solaris, Novell.NetWare, MacOSX, Mi crosoft Windows, OS/2, TPF, OpenVMS andeComStation.
Released under the Apache License, Apache is open-source software.

As of June 2013, Apache was estimated to serve 54.2% of all active Web sites and 53.3% of the top servers across all domains.

Here's a list other important and popular web servers:

Apache Tomcat
The Apache Tomcat has been developed to support servlets and JSP scripts. Though it can serve as a standalone server, Tomcat is generally used along with the popular Apache HTTP web server or any other web server. Apache Tomcat is free and open source and can run on different operating systems like Linux, Unix, Windows, Mac OS X, Free BSD.

Microsoft's Internet Information Services (IIS) Windows Server
IIS Windows Web Server has been developed by the software giant, Microsoft. It offers higher levels of performance and security than its predecessors. It also comes with a good support from the company and is the second most popular server on the web.

Nginx web server
Free open source popular web server including IMAP/POP3 proxy server. Hosting about 7.5% of all domains worldwide, Nginx is known for its high performance, stability, simple configuration and low resource usage. This web server doesn't use threads to handle requests rather a much more scalable event-driven architecture which uses small and predictable amounts of memory under load.

Lighttpd

lighttpd, pronounced "lighty" (don't ask me why), is a free web server distributed with the FreeBSD operating system. This open source web server is fast, secure and consumes much less CPU power. Lighttpd can also run on Windows, Mac OS X, Linux and Solaris operating systems.

Jigsaw

Jigsaw (W3C's Server) comes from the World Wide Web Consortium. It is open source and free and can run on various platforms like Linux, Unix, Windows, Mac OS X Free BSD etc.

Jigsaw has been written in Java and can run CGI scripts and PHP programs.

Klone

Klone, from KoanLogic Srl, includes a web server and an SDK for creating static and dynamic web sites.

It is a web application development framework especially for embedded systems and appliances.No additional components are required when using Klone; thus, one can do away with an HTTP/S server or the active pages engine (PHP, Perl, ASP).

Abyss web server

Abyss compact web server runs on all popular platforms - Windows, Mac OS X, Linux and FreeBSD. The personal edition is (X1) 100% free while the professional Abyss Web Server X2 has a small price tag of $60.

Supports HTTP/1.1, secure connections, CGI/FastCGI, custom error pages, password protection and much more. The server also has an automatic antihacking system and a multiligual remote web management   interface.

Oracle Web Tier

Includes two web server options with reverse proxy and caching solutions that lead to quick serving of web pages and easy handling of even the most demanding http traffic.

The iPlanet Web Server, for example, is a high-performance server with enhanced security and mutithreaded archictecture that scales well on modern 64-bit multiprocessors.

X5 (Xitami) web server

The cross-platform X5 from iMatrix Corporation is the latest generation web server using the company's own multithreading technology (Base2) that makes it scalable to multi cores.

As per the iMatrix, X5 can handle thousands of connections without difficulty and thus is useful for long polling in which connections from clients remain open for extended durations.

Zeus web server

The Zeus web server runs on Linux and Free BSD operating systems among others. It has been developed by Zeus technology Ltd. And is known for its speed, reliability, security and flexibility. The web server is used on some of the busiest web sites of the world including Ebay. Zeus web server is *not free* and costs more than a thousand pounds.

LAMP Server

Introduction

A "LAMP" stack is a group of open source software that is typically installed together to enable a server to host dynamic web-sites and web apps. This term is actually an acronym which represents the Linux Operating System, with the Apache web server. The site data is stored in a MySQL database, and dynamic content is processed by PHP.

Now, we'll get a LAMP stack installed on an Ubuntu 14.04 .01 VPS. Ubuntu will fulfill our first requirement: a Linux Operating System.

Prerequisites
Before you begin with the next steps, you should have a separate, non-root user account set up on your server.

Install Apache
The Apache web server is currently the most popular web server in the world, which makes it a great default choice for hosting a web-site. We can install Apache easily using Ubuntu's package manager, apt. A package manager allows us to install most soft-ware pain-free from a repository maintained by Ubuntu.

For our purposes, we can get started by typing these commands:

sudo apt-get update
sudo apt-get install apache2

Since we are using a *sudo* command, these operations get executed with root privileges. It will ask you for your regular user's password to verify your intentions.

Afterwards, the web server is installed. You can do a spot check right away to verify that everything went as planned by visiting your server's public IP address in your web browser:

http://server-IP-address

You will see the default Ubuntu 14.04 Apache web page, which is there for informational and testing purposes. It should look something like this:

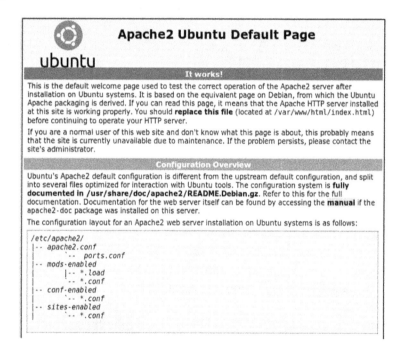

If you see this page, then your web server is now correctly installed.

Install MySQL

Now that we have our web server up and running, it is time to install MySQL. MySQL is a database management system. Basically, it will organize and provide access to databases where our site can store information.

Again, we can use apt to acquire and install our software. This time, we'll also install some other "helper" packages that will assist us in getting our components to communicate with each other:

sudo apt-get install mysql-server php5-mysql

Note: In this case, you do not have to run *sudo apt-get update* prior to the command. This is because we recently ran it in the commands above to install Apache. The package index on our computer should already be up-to-date.

During the installation, your server will ask you to select and confirm a password for the MySQL *"root"* user. This is an administrative account in MySQL that has increased privileges. Think of it as being similar to the root account for the server itself (the one you are configuring now is a MySQL-specific account however).

When the installation is complete, we need to run some additional commands to get our MySQL environment set up securely.

First, we need to tell MySQL to create its database directory structure where it will store its information. You can do this by typing:

sudo mysql_install_db

Afterwards, we want to run a simple security script that will remove some dangerous defaults and lock down access to our database system a little bit.

Start the interactive script by running:

sudo mysql_secure_installation

You will be asked to enter the password you set for the MySQL root account. Next, it will ask you if you want to change that password. If you are happy with your current password, type "*n*" for "no" at the prompt.

For the rest of the questions, you should simply hit the "ENTER" key through each prompt to accept the default values. This will remove some sample users and databases, disable remote root logins, and load these new rules so that MySQL immediately respects the changes we have made.

Install PHP
PHP is the component of our setup that will process code to display dynamic content. It can run scripts, connect to our MySQL databases to get information, and hand the processed content over to our web server to display.

We can once again leverage the apt system to install our components. We're going to include some helper packages as well:

sudo apt-get install php5 libapache2-mod-php5 php5-mcrypt

This should install PHP without any problems. We'll test this in a moment. In most cases, we'll want to modify the way that Apache serves files when a directory is requested. Currently, if a user requests a directory from the server, Apache will first look for a file calledindex.html. We want to tell our web server to prefer PHP files, so we'll make Apache look for anindex.php file first.
To do this, type this command to open the *dir.conf* file in a text editor with root privileges:

sudo nano /etc/apache2/mods-enabled/dir.conf

It will look like this:

<IfModule mod_dir.c>
  DirectoryIndex index.html index.cgi index.pl index.php
idenx.xhtml index.htm
</IfModule>

We want to move the PHP index file highlighted above to the first position after theDirectoryIndex specification, like this:

<IfModule mod_dir.c>
  DirectoryIndex   index.php   index.html   index.cgi   index.pl
idenx.xhtml index.htm
</IfModule>

When you are finished, save and close the file by pressing "CTRL+x". You'll have to confirm the save by typing "*y*" and then hit "Enter" to confirm the file save location.

After this, we need to restart the Apache web server in order for our changes to be recognized. You can do this by typing this:

sudo service apache2 restart

Install PHP Modules
To enhance the functionality of PHP, we can optionally install some additional modules.

To see the available options for PHP modules and libraries, you can type this into your system:

apt-cache search php5-

The results are all optional components that you can install. It will give you a short description for each:

php5-cgi - server-side, HTML-embedded scripting language (CGI binary)
php5-cli - command-line interpreter for the php5 scripting language
php5-common - Common files for packages built from the php5 source
php5-curl - CURL module for php5
php5-dbg - Debug symbols for PHP5
php5-dev - Files for PHP5 module development
php5-gd - GD module for php5
. . .

To get more information about what each module does, you can either search the internet, or you can look at the long description in the package by typing:

apt-cache show package_name

There will be a lot of output, with one field called Description-en which will have a longer explanation of the functionality that the module provides.
For example, to find out what the php5-cli module does, we could type this:

apt-cache show php5-cli

Along with a large amount of other information, you'll find something that looks like this:

...
SHA256:
91cfdbda65df65c9a4a5bd3478d6e7d3e92c53efcddf3436bbe9bbe27eca409d
Description-en: command-line interpreter for the php5 scripting language

This package provides the /usr/bin/php5 command interpreter, useful for testing PHP scripts from a shell or performing general shell scripting tasks.

.

The following extensions are built in: bcmath bz2 calendar Core ctype date dba dom ereg exif fileinfo filter ftp gettext hash iconv libxml mbstring mhash openssl pcntl pcre Phar posix Reflection session shmop SimpleXML soap sockets SPL standard sysvmsg sysvsem sysvshm tokenizer wddx xml xmlreader xmlwriter zip zlib.

.

PHP (recursive acronym for PHP: Hypertext Preprocessor) is a widely-used open source general-purpose scripting language that is especially suited for web development and can be embedded into HTML.
Description-md5: f8450d3b28653dcf1a4615f3b1d4e347
Homepage: http://www.php.net/
. . .

If, after researching, you decide you would like to install a package, you can do so by using the apt-get install command like we have been doing for our other software.
If we decided that php5-cli is something that we need, we could type:

sudo apt-get install php5-cli

If you want to install more than one module, you can do that by listing each one, separated by a space, following the apt-get install command, like this:

sudo apt-get install package1 package2 ...

At this point, your LAMP stack is installed and configured. We should still test out our PHP though.

Test PHP Processing on your Web Server
In order to test that our system is configured properly for PHP, we can create a very basic PHP script.

We will call this script info.php. In order for Apache to find the file and serve it correctly, it must be saved to a very specific directory, which is called the "web root".

In Ubuntu Server 14.04 LTS, this directory is located at */var/www/html/*.
We can create the file at that location by typing:

sudo nano /var/www/html/info.php

This will open a blank file. We want to put the following text, which is valid PHP code, inside the file:

<?php
phpinfo();
?>

When you are finished, save and close the file. A good rule is to be the owner and right chmod the file; supposing our preferred user is 'webmaster' or (just use the default user 'www-data' instead):

sudo chown webmaster:www-data info.php

sudo chmod 644 info.php

Now we can test whether our web server can correctly display content generated by a PHP script.

To try this out, we just have to visit this page in our web browser. You'll need your server's public IP address again. The address you want to visit will be:

http://your_server_IP_address/info.php

The page that you come to should look something like this:

PHP Version 5.5.9-1ubuntu4	php

System	Linux blah 3.13.0-24-generic #46-Ubuntu SMP Thu Apr 10 19:11:08 UTC 2014 x86_64
Build Date	Apr 9 2014 17:08:00
Server API	Apache 2.0 Handler
Virtual Directory Support	disabled
Configuration File (php.ini) Path	/etc/php5/apache2
Loaded Configuration File	/etc/php5/apache2/php.ini
Scan this dir for additional .ini files	/etc/php5/apache2/conf.d
Additional .ini files parsed	/etc/php5/apache2/conf.d/05-opcache.ini, /etc/php5/apache2/conf.d/10-pdo.ini, /etc/php5/apache2/conf.d/20-json.ini, /etc/php5/apache2/conf.d/20-mysql.ini, /etc/php5/apache2/conf.d/20-mysqli.ini, /etc/php5/apache2/conf.d/20-pdo_mysql.ini, /etc/php5/apache2/conf.d/20-readline.ini
PHP API	20121113
PHP Extension	20121212
Zend Extension	220121212
Zend Extension Build	API220121212,NTS
PHP Extension Build	API20121212,NTS

This page basically gives you information about your server from the perspective of PHP. It is useful for debugging and to ensure that your settings are being applied correctly. If this was successful, then your PHP is working as expected.

You probably want to remove this file after this test because it could actually give information about your server to unauthorized users. To do this, you can type this:

sudo rm /var/www/html/info.php

You can always recreate this page if you need to access the information again later.

Tip: a short time secure solution wanting to leave info.php placed on the server is to add on it an authentication form; the file will be:

```php
<?php
// Define your username and password
$username = "MYUSERNAME"; $password = "MYPASSWORD"; if
($_POST['txtUsername'] != $username || $_POST['txtPassword'] != $pass-
word) { ?>
<center><h1>Login</h1>  <form  name="form"  method="post"  ac-
tion="<?php echo $_SERVER['PHP_SELF']; ?>">
   <p><label for="txtUsername">Username:</label>
   <br /><input type="text" title="Enter your Username" name="txtUsername"
/></p>
   <p><label for="txtpassword">Password:</label>
   <br  /><input  type="password"  title="Enter  your  password"
name="txtPassword" /></p>
   <p><input  type="submit"  name="Submit"  value="Login"  /></p>
</form></center> <?php
}
else {
?>
<?php phpinfo();
}
?>
```

substitute MYUSERNAME and MYPASSWORD with what you pre-fer.

Apache Virtual Hosts

Apache breaks its functionality and components into individual units that can be customized and configured independently. The basic unit that describes an individual site or domain is called virtual host.

These designations allow the administrator to use one server to host multiple domains or sites off of a single interface or IP by using a matching mechanism. This is relevant to anyone looking to host more than one site off of a single VPS.

Each domain that is configured will direct the visitor to a specific directory holding that site's information, never indicating that the same server is also responsible for other sites. This scheme is expandable without any software limit as long as your server can handle the load.

In the next steps, we will walk you through how to set up Apache virtual hosts on an Ubuntu Server 14.04 LTS VPS. During this process, you'll learn how to serve different content to different visitors depending on which domains they are requesting.

Prerequisites

Before you begin this tutorial, you should create a non-root user.

You will also need to have Apache installed in order to work through these steps.

The proposed configuration will make a virtual host for *example.com* and another for *test.com* but you should substitute your own domains or values while following along.

If you do *not* have domains available to play with, you can use dummy values.

We will show how to edit your local hosts file later on to test the configuration if you are using dummy values. This will allow you to test your configuration from your home computer, even though your content won't be available through the domain name to other visitors.

Create the Directory Structure

The first step that we are going to take is to make a directory structure that will hold the site data that we will be serving to visitors.
Our document root (the top-level directory that Apache looks at to find content to serve) will be set to individual directories under the */var/www directory*. We will create a directory here for both of the virtual hosts we plan on making.

Within each of these directories, we will create a public_html file that will hold our actual files. This gives us some flexibility in our hosting.
For instance, for our sites, we're going to make our directories like this:

sudo mkdir -p /var/www/example.com/public_html
sudo mkdir -p /var/www/test.com/public_html

Grant Permissions

Now there is the directory structure for our files, but they are owned by our root user. If we want our regular user to be able to modify files in our web directories, we can change the ownership by doing this:

sudo chown -R $USER:$USER /var/www/example.com/public_html

sudo chown -R $USER:$USER /var/www/test.com/public_html

The $USER variable will take the value of the user you are currently logged in as when you press "ENTER". By doing this, our regular user now owns the public_html subdirectories where we will be storing our content.

We should also modify our permissions a little bit to ensure that read access is permitted to the general web directory and all of the files and folders it contains so that pages can be served correctly:

sudo chmod -R 755 /var/www

Your web server should now have the permissions it needs to serve content, and your user should be able to create content within the necessary folders.

Create Demo Pages for Each Virtual Host
We have our directory structure in place. Let's create some content to serve. We're just going for a demonstration, so our pages will be very simple. We're just going to make anindex.html page for each site.

Let's start with example.com. We can open up an index.html file in our editor by typing:

nano /var/www/example.com/public_html/index.html

In this file, create a simple HTML document that indicates the site it is connected to. My file looks like this:

```
<html>
 <head>
  <title>Welcome to Example.com!</title>
 </head>
 <body>
  <h1>Success!  The example.com virtual host is working!</h1>
 </body>
</html>
```

Save and close the file when you are finished.
We can copy this file to use as the basis for our second site by typing:

cp /var/www/example.com/public_html/index.html
/var/www/test.com/public_html/index.html

We can then open the file and modify the relevant pieces of information:

nano /var/www/test.com/public_html/index.html
<html>
<head>
<title>Welcome to Test.com!</title>
</head>
<body>
<h1>Success! The test.com virtual host is working!</h1>
</body>
</html>

Save and close this file as well. Here's now the pages necessary to test the virtual host configuration.

Create New Virtual Host Files
Virtual host files are the files that specify the actual configuration of our virtual hosts and dictate how the Apache web server will respond to various domain requests.
Apache comes with a default virtual host file called *000-default.conf* that we can use as a jumping off point. We are going to copy it over to create a virtual host file for each of our domains.
The virtual hosts configuration allows to aim the subdomains as well (e.g. subdomain1.example.com, subdomain2.test.com, etc.).
We're going to start with one domain, configure it, copy it for our second domain, and then make the few further adjustments needed.

50

The default Ubuntu configuration requires that each virtual host file end in .conf.

Create the First Virtual Host File. Start by copying the file for the first domain:

sudo cp /etc/apache2/sites-available/000-default.conf
/etc/apache2/sites-available/example.com.conf

Open the new file in your editor with root privileges:

sudo nano /etc/apache2/sites-available/example.com.conf

The file will look something like this (I've removed the comments here to make the file more approachable):

*<VirtualHost *:80>*
*   ServerAdmin webmaster@localhost*
*   DocumentRoot /var/www/html*
*   ErrorLog ${APACHE_LOG_DIR}/error.log*
*   CustomLog ${APACHE_LOG_DIR}/access.log combined*
</VirtualHost>

As you can see, there's not much here. We will customize the items here for our first domain and add some additional directives. This virtual host section matches *any* requests that are made on port 80, the default HTTP port.
First, we need to change the ServerAdmin directive to an email that the site administrator can receive emails through:

ServerAdmin admin@example.com

After this, we need to *add* two directives. The first, called ServerName, establishes the base domain that should match for this virtual host definition. This will most likely be your domain. The second, called ServerAlias, defines further names that should match as if they were the base name. This is useful for matching hosts you defined, like www:

ServerName example.com
ServerAlias www.example.com

The only other thing we need to change for a basic virtual host file is the location of the document root for this domain. We already created the directory we need, so we just need to alter the DocumentRoot directive to reflect the directory we created:

DocumentRoot /var/www/example.com/public_html

In total, our virtualhost file should look like this:

*<VirtualHost *:80>*
 ServerAdmin admin@example.com
 ServerName example.com
 ServerAlias www.example.com
 DocumentRoot /var/www/example.com/public_html
 ErrorLog ${APACHE_LOG_DIR}/error.log
 CustomLog ${APACHE_LOG_DIR}/access.log combined
</VirtualHost>

Save and close the file.

Copy First Virtual Host and Customize for Second Domain
Now that we have our first virtual host file established, we can create our second one by copying that file and adjusting it as needed. Start by copying it:

sudo cp /etc/apache2/sites-available/example.com.conf
/etc/apache2/sites-available/test.com.conf

Open the new file with root privileges in your editor:

sudo nano /etc/apache2/sites-available/test.com.conf

You now need to modify all of the pieces of information to reference your second domain. When you are finished, it may look something like this:

*<VirtualHost *:80>*
 ServerAdmin admin@test.com
 ServerName test.com
 ServerAlias www.test.com
 DocumentRoot /var/www/test.com/public_html
 ErrorLog ${APACHE_LOG_DIR}/error.log
 CustomLog ${APACHE_LOG_DIR}/access.log combined
</VirtualHost>

Save and close the file when you are finished.

Enable the New Virtual Host Files
Now that we have created our virtual host files, we must enable them. Apache includes some tools that allow us to do this.
We can use the a2ensite tool to enable each of our sites like this:

sudo a2ensite example.com.conf
sudo a2ensite test.com.conf

When you are finished, you need to restart Apache to make these changes take effect:

sudo service apache2 restart

Don't care about some harmless message that does not affect our site.

If you followed along, you should now have a single server handling two separate domain names. You can expand this process by following the steps we outlined above to make additional virtual hosts – really, there isn't software limit on the number of domain names Apache Web Server can handle.

SSL Certificates on Apache Web Server

Introduction
TLS, or transport layer security, and its predecessor *SSL*, secure sockets layer, are secure protocols created in order to place normal traffic in a protected, encrypted wrapper.

These protocols allow traffic to be sent safely between remote parties without the possibility of the traffic being intercepted and read by someone in the middle. They are also instrumental in validating the identity of domains and servers throughout the internet by establishing a server as trusted and genuine by a certificate authority.

We will cover how to create a *self-signed SSL certificate* for Apache on an Ubuntu Server 14.04 LTS, which will allow you to encrypt traffic to your server. While this does not provide the benefit of third party validation of your server's identity, it fulfills the requirements of those simply wanting to transfer information securely.

Prerequisites
Before you begin, you should have some configuration already taken care of.

We will be operating as a non-root user with *sudo* privileges.

Activate the SSL Module
SSL support actually comes standard in the Ubuntu 14.04 Apache package. We simply need to enable it to take advantage of SSL on our system.

Enable the module by typing:

sudo a2enmod ssl

After you have enabled SSL, you'll have to restart the web server for the change to be recognized:

sudo service apache2 restart

With that, our web server is now able to handle SSL if we configure it to do so.

Create a Self-Signed SSL Certificate
First of first is clear, if you bought an SSL certificate from an Authorized Certificate Authority the next steps can be jumped, otherwise wanting to create a self signed certificate let's start off by creating a subdirectory within Apache's configuration hierarchy to place the certificate files that we will be making:

sudo mkdir /etc/apache2/ssl

Now that we have a location to place our key and certificate, we can create them both in one step by typing:

sudo openssl req -x509 -nodes -days 365 -newkey rsa:2048 -keyout /etc/apache2/ssl/apache.key -out /etc/apache2/ssl/apache.crt

Let's go over exactly what this means:

- **openssl**: This is the basic command line tool provided by OpenSSL to create and manage certificates, keys, signing requests, etc.
- **req**: This specifies a subcommand for X.509 certificate signing request (CSR) management. X.509 is a public key infrastructure standard that SSL adheres to for its key and certificate managment. Since we are wanting to *create* a new X.509 certificate, this is what we want.
- **-x509**: This option specifies that we want to make a self-signed certificate file instead of generating a certificate request.

VPS TOOLKIT

- **-nodes**: This option tells OpenSSL that we do not wish to secure our key file with a passphrase. Having a password protected key file would get in the way of Apache starting automatically as we would have to enter the password every time the service restarts.
- **-days 365**: This specifies that the certificate we are creating will be valid for one year.
- **-newkey rsa:2048**: This option will create the certificate request and a new private key at the same time. This is necessary since we didn't create a private key in advance. The rsa:2048tells OpenSSL to generate an RSA key that is 2048 bits long.
- **-keyout**: This parameter names the output file for the private key file that is being created.
- **-out**: This option names the output file for the certificate that we are generating.

When you hit "ENTER", you will be asked a number of questions. The most important item that is requested is the line that reads "Common Name (e.g. server FQDN or YOUR name)". You should enter the domain name you want to associate with the certificate, or the server's public IP address if you do not have a domain name.

The questions portion looks something like this:

Country Name (2 letter code) [AU]:US
State or Province Name (full name) [Some-State]:New York
Locality Name (eg, city) []:New York City
Organization Name (eg, company) [Internet Widgits Pty Ltd]:Your Company
Organizational Unit Name (eg, section) []:Department of Kittens
Common Name (e.g. server FQDN or YOUR name) []:your_domain.com
Email Address []:your_email@domain.com

The key and certificate will be created and placed in your */etc/apache2/ssl* directory.

Configure Apache to Use SSL

Now that we have our certificate and key available, we can configure Apache to use these files in a virtual host file.

Instead of basing our configuration file off of the *000-default.conf* file in the sites-available subdirectory, we're going to base this configuration on the *default-ssl.conf* file that contains some default SSL configuration.

Open the file with root privileges now:

sudo nano /etc/apache2/sites-available/default-ssl.conf

With the comments removed, the file looks something like this:

```
<IfModule mod_ssl.c>
        <VirtualHost _default_:443>
                ServerAdmin webmaster@localhost
                DocumentRoot /var/www/html
                ErrorLog ${APACHE_LOG_DIR}/error.log
                CustomLog ${APACHE_LOG_DIR}/access.log combined
                SSLEngine on
                SSLCertificateFile /etc/ssl/certs/ssl-cert-snakeoil.pem
                SSLCertificateKeyFile /etc/ssl/private/ssl-cert-snakeoil.key
        <FilesMatch "\.(cgi|shtml|phtml|php)$">
                SSLOptions +StdEnvVars
        </FilesMatch>
        <Directory /usr/lib/cgi-bin>
                SSLOptions +StdEnvVars
        </Directory>
                BrowserMatch "MSIE [2-6]" \
                nokeepalive ssl-unclean-shutdown \
                downgrade-1.0 force-response-1.0
                BrowserMatch "MSIE [17-9]" ssl-unclean-shutdown
        </VirtualHost>
</IfModule>
```

This may look a bit complicated, but luckily, we don't need to worry about most of the options here.

We want to set the normal things we'd configure for a virtual host (ServerAdmin, ServerName, ServerAlias, DocumentRoot, etc.) as well as change the location where Apache looks for the SSL certificate and key.

In the end, it will look something like this. The entries in red were modified from the original file:

```
<IfModule mod_ssl.c>
        <VirtualHost _default_:443>
                ServerAdmin admin@example.com
                ServerName your_domain.com
                ServerAlias www.your_domain.com
                DocumentRoot /var/www/html
                ErrorLog ${APACHE_LOG_DIR}/error.log
                CustomLog ${APACHE_LOG_DIR}/access.log combined
                SSLEngine on
                SSLCertificateFile /etc/apache2/ssl/apache.crt
                SSLCertificateKeyFile /etc/apache2/ssl/apache.key
        <FilesMatch "\.(cgi|shtml|phtml|php)$">
                SSLOptions +StdEnvVars
        </FilesMatch>
        <Directory /usr/lib/cgi-bin>
                SSLOptions +StdEnvVars
        </Directory>
                BrowserMatch "MSIE [2-6]" \
                nokeepalive ssl-unclean-shutdown \
                downgrade-1.0 force-response-1.0
                BrowserMatch "MSIE [17-9]" ssl-unclean-shutdown
        </VirtualHost>
</IfModule>
```

Save and exit the file when you are finished.

Activate the SSL Virtual Host

Now that we have configured our SSL-enabled virtual host, we need to enable it. We can do this by typing:

sudo a2ensite default-ssl.conf

We then need to restart Apache to load our new virtual host file:

sudo service apache2 restart

This should enable your new virtual host, which will serve encrypted content using the SSL certificate you created.

Testing

Now that you have everything prepared, you can test your configuration by visiting your server's domain name or public IP address after specifying the https:// protocol, like this:

https://server_domain_name_or_IP

You will get a warning that your browser cannot verify the identity of your server because it has not been signed by one of the certificate authorities that it trusts.

This is expected since we have self-signed our certificate. While our certificate will not validate our server for our users because it has had no interaction with a trusted certificate authority, it will still be able to encrypt communication.

Since this is expected, you can hit the "Proceed anyway" button or whatever similar option you have in your browser.

You will now be taken to content in the DocumentRoot that you configured for your SSL virtual host. This time your traffic is encrypted. You can check this by clicking on the lock icon in the menu bar:

You can see in the middle green section that the connection is encrypted.

You should now have SSL enabled on your website. This will help to secure communication between visitors and your site, but it *will* warn each user that the browser cannot verify the validity of the certificate.

If you are planning on launching a public site and need SSL, you will be better off purchasing an SSL certificate from a trusted certificate authority.

VPS TOOLKIT

:: 4:: VPS Components

DNS Server

Introduction
Domain Name Service (DNS) is an Internet service that maps IP addresses and fully qualified domain names (FQDN) to one another. In this way, DNS alleviates the need to remember IP addresses. Computers that run DNS are called name servers. Ubuntu ships with BIND (Berkley Internet Naming Daemon), the most widely deployed DNS server. This guide is aimed at people looking to learn how to configure and maintain a DNS server, such as for a network (caching name server) or to serve DNS zones for a domain name.

Installation
In a VPS environment BIND should come with the default configuration, if not to install it just type:

sudo apt-get install bind9

this way BIND9 is ready to work can serve the VPS throw its current internet connection and its network interfaces. A very useful package for testing and troubleshooting DNS issues is the *dnsutils* package; to install it:

sudo apt-get install dnsutils

for our purpose now the BIND9 configuration is finished. A step ahead could be to set up an authoritative-only DNS server. It only respond to iterative queries for the zones that they are authoritative for. This means that if the server does not know the answer, it will just tell the client (usually some kind of resolving DNS server) that it does not know the answer and give a reference to a server that may know more. Authoritative-only DNS servers are often a good configuration for high performance because they do not have the overhead of resolving recursive queries from clients. They only care about the zones that they are designed to serve.

Other possible configuration scenarios
BIND9 can provide many different DNS services. Some of the most useful setups are:

:: Caching Server ::
In this configuration BIND9 will find the answer to name queries and remember the answer for the next query. This can be useful for a slow internet connection. By caching DNS queries, you will reduce bandwidth and (more importantly) latency.

:: Primary Master Server ::
BIND9 can be used to serve DNS records (groups of records are referred to as zones) for a registered domain name or an imaginary one (but only if used on a restricted network).

:: Secondary Master Server ::
A secondary master DNS server is used to complement a primary master DNS server by serving a copy of the zone(s) configured on the primary server. Secondary servers are recommended in larger setups. If you intend to serve a registered domain name they ensure that your DNS zone is still available even if your primary server is not online.

:: Hybrids ::
You can even configure BIND9 to be a Caching and Primary Master DNS server simultaneously, a Caching and a Secondary Master server or even a Caching, Primary Master and Secondary Master

server. All that is required is simply combining the different con-figuration examples.

:: Stealth Servers ::

There are also two other common DNS server setups (used when working with zones for registered domain names), Stealth Primary and Stealth Secondary. These are effectively the same as Primary and Secondary DNS servers, but with a slight organizational difference. For example, you have 3 DNS servers; A, B and C. A is the Primary, B and C are secondaries. If you configure your registered domain to use A and B as your domain's DNS servers, then C is a Stealth Secondary. It's still a secondary, but it's not going to be asked about the zone you are serving to the internet from A and B If you configure your registered domain to use B and C as your domain's DNS servers, then A is a stealth primary. Any additional records or edits to the zone are done on A, but computers on the internet will only ever ask B and C about the zone.

MAIL Server

Introduction

Just to be clear, there's no reason for to create a mail server on VPS to manage our own emails. This because the very limited disk space and also to avoid to affect its resources. Instead, we desire to allow the VPS to send system emails, often utilizing the power of PHP and its capabilities.

Sendmail

To allow the php applications to be able to send our email using the mail function we need to install *sendmail* and enable it to the *php.ini* file:

sudo apt-get install sendmail

check its working:
ps -aux | grep sendmail

modify the php.ini file:

sudo nano /etc/php5/apache2/php.ini

replacing: *;sendmail_path =*
with: *sendmail_path = /usr/sbin/sendmail*

now Sendmail is configured to send email locally, so you need to edit the config file:

sudo nano /etc/mail/sendmail.mc

adding these lines to the bottom (where example is your domain name):

define(`MAIL_HUB', `example.com.')
dnl define(`LOCAL_RELAY', `example.com.')dnl

to make the configuration taking place just run:

sudo sendmailconfig

answering 'yes' on every question and confirming to maintain the current configuration, then restart the service

sudo service sendmail restart

to test Sendmail from the Terminal:

echo -e "To: user@example.com\nSubject: Test\nTest\n" | sendmail -bm -t -v

FTP Server

ProFTP Server

ProFTPD is a popular ftp server. Because it was written as a power-ful and configurable program, it is not necessarily the lightest ftp server available for virtual servers.

Warning!
FTP is extremely not secure!

..but it's also true that's the most used method to transfer file In&Out to an hosting space.

Installation

The fast way to install ProFTP on the VPS is by the command line:

sudo apt-get install proftpd

While the file is installing, you will be given the choice to run your VPS as an *inetd* or *standalone* server. Choose the standalone op-tion.

After this, we still have to make a few changes to the configuration.

Configuration

Once ProFTPD is installed, you can make the needed adjustments in the configuration. Unlike some other FTP configurations, ProFTPD disables anonymous login from the outset and we only need to make a couple of alterations in the config file. Open up the file:

sudo nano /etc/proftpd/proftpd.conf

change the server's name to your host-name:

ServerName   example.com

uncomment the line that says *Default Root*. Doing so will limit users to their home directory:

 # Use this to jail all users in their homes DefaultRoot   ~

Then save & exit.

Restart after all of your changes:

sudo service proftpd restart

Improve the security
Configure ProFTPd to use SFTP instead of FTP

FTP, or File Transfer Protocol, is a popular way to transfer files between local and remote servers. While FTP was a preferred method of transfer in the past, it authenticates in plain text, making it insecure. ProFTPd is a popular FTP server that can be configured to use the SFTP protocol, a secure FTP alternative, instead of FTP.

Configure SFTP Access with ProFTPd

The default file looks in the *conf.d* subdirectory for additional configuration. We will create a file there to enable the use of SFTP:

sudo nano /etc/proftpd/conf.d/sftp.conf

ProFTPd can take configuration with the same formatting as Apache and it's easy to figure out. Copy and paste the following into the file:

69

```
<IfModule mod_sftp.c>

    SFTPEngine on
    Port 2222
    SFTPLog /var/log/proftpd/sftp.log

    # Configure both the RSA and DSA host keys, using the same host key
    # files that OpenSSH uses.
    SFTPHostKey /etc/ssh/ssh_host_rsa_key
    SFTPHostKey /etc/ssh/ssh_host_dsa_key

    SFTPAuthMethods publickey

    SFTPAuthorizedUserKeys file:/etc/proftpd/authorized_keys/%u

    # Enable compression
    SFTPCompression delayed

</IfModule>
```

Deconstructing the SFTP Configuration

Let's break the file down into its component pieces so that we can understand it better. The entire section is wrapped in *IfModule* tags to make sure that the configuration options are only applied if the SFTP module is available (which it is);

SFTPEngine on: Enables the SFTP ability for the server *Port 2222*: Specifies the port where the SFTP connections will be accepted. Since SSH already is looking for connections on port 22, we want a different port.

SFTPLog: Configures the location of the log file that will be created.

SFTPHostKey: These two lines point to the SSH host keys. This is how the server identifies itself to clients. For the most part, the lines we used should be correct.

SFTPAuthMethods: This line configures the server to only accept connections with SSH keys.

SFTPAuthorizedUserKeys: This parameter names the location of the SFTP keys that can be used to authenticate someone. The %u portion will substitute the authenticating user's name.

SFTPCompression delayed: This sets the compression mechanism that will be utilized during file transfers.

Configure Key Based Authentication
The ProFTPd can use SSH keys to authenticate users, but the keys must be converted to use the RFC4716 format. Luckily, the SSH suite has the ability to convert these files natively. Begin by creating a directory to house these files:

sudo mkdir /etc/proftpd/authorized_keys

Now, we need to convert the public keys that are currently used to log into the server. If you only have one user, you can use this command:

sudo ssh-keygen -e -f ~username/.ssh/authorized_keys | sudo tee /etc/proftpd/authorized_keys/username

If you have multiple users and you need to separate their log in credentials, you will have to use the actual public key instead of the authorized_keys file, like this:

sudo ssh-keygen -e -f /path/to/id_rsa.pub | sudo tee /etc/proftpd/authorized_keys/username_who_owns_key

You can add as many keys as you would like. When you are finished, restart the ProFTPd server:

sudo service proftpd restart

Disable SFTP Access on the SSH Port
Now that we have enabled SFTP through ProFTPd, we can disable it on the normal SSH port. This will allow us to configure user access and lock down what each user can see and manipulate through ProFTPd, without worrying about people being able to leave their home directories. Open the SSHD configuration file:

sudo nano /etc/ssh/sshd_config

towards the bottom of the file, you should see a line that looks like this:

Subsystem sftp /usr/lib/openssh/sftp-server

Put a hash (#) in front of it to comment out the line:

 # Subsystem sftp /usr/lib/openssh/sftp-server

and then, save and close the file.

Now, restart the SSH server so to enable your changes:

sudo service ssh restart

connecting with a Client There are plenty of FTP clients that we can use to connect with our server. The good ones implement SFTP capabilities as well, ie FileZilla, CyberDuck, etc.

:: 5 :: Web Applications

Introduction

When the VPS is ready to go and serve to the internet its capabilities it's time to add the contents on it. This is the moment we'll really appreciate the fact that the work will be very fast, avoiding for instance long times uploading files throw FTP or chmod-ing entire folders; in fact now it's possible to do this kind of routine operations just in a moment and also more, having the full control of the web server and all the processes running on it.

Let's install some useful and so famous applications.

phpMyadmin

To feel more comfortable interacting with the system using a GUI instead from the MySQL prompt, phpMyadmin is a good choice.

Installation

To get started, we can simply install phpMyAdmin from the default Ubuntu repositories,

sudo apt-get install phpmyadmin

this will ask you a few questions in order to configure your installation correctly:

- for the server selection, choose *apache2*. Note: If you do not hit "SPACE" to select Apache, the installer will not move the necessary files during installation. Hit "SPACE", "TAB", and then "ENTER" to select Apache;

- select yes when asked whether to use *dbconfig-common* to set up the database;
- you will be prompted for your database administrator's password;
- you will then be asked to choose and confirm a password for the phpMyAdmin application itself.

The installation process actually adds the phpMyAdmin Apache configuration file into the */etc/apache2/conf-enabled/* directory, where it is automatically read.
The only thing we need to do is explicitly enable the *php5-mcrypt extension*, which we can do by typing:

sudo php5enmod mcrypt

phpMyAdmin

Welcome to phpMyAdmin

Language

English ▼

Log In

Username:

Password:

Go

Afterwards, restart Apache for the changes to be recognized:

sudo service apache2 restart

Now access the web interface by visiting your server's domain name or public IP address followed by */phpmyadmin*:

http://domain_name_or_IP/phpmyadmin

You can now log into the interface using the root username and the administrative password you set up during the MySQL installation.

Secure the phpMyAdmin Instance

We were able to get our phpMyAdmin interface up and running fairly easily. However, we are not done yet. Because of its ubiquity, phpMyAdmin is a popular target for attackers. We need to secure the application to help prevent unauthorized use.

One of the easiest way of doing this is to place a gateway in front of the entire application. We can do this using Apache's built-in *.htaccess* authentication and authorization functionalities.

Configure Apache to Allow .htaccess Overrides

First, we need to enable the use of *.htaccess* file overrides by editing our Apache configuration file. We will edit the linked file that has been placed in our Apache configuration directory:

sudo nano /etc/apache2/conf-available/phpmyadmin.conf

We need to add an AllowOverride All directive within the *<Directory /usr/share/phpmyadmin>* section of the configuration file, like this:

<Directory /usr/share/phpmyadmin>
  Options FollowSymLinks
  DirectoryIndex index.php
  AllowOverride All
  . . .

When you have added this line, save and close the file.
To implement the changes you made, restart Apache:

sudo service apache2 restart

Create an .htaccess file
Now that we have enabled *.htaccess* use for our application, we
need to create one to actually implement some security.
In order for this to be successful, the file must be created within the
application directory. We can create the necessary file and open it
in our text editor with root privileges by typing:

sudo nano /usr/share/phpmyadmin/.htaccess

Within this file, we need to enter the following information:

AuthType Basic
AuthName "Restricted Files"
AuthUserFile /etc/phpmyadmin/.htpasswd

Require valid-user
Let's go over what each of these lines mean:

- **AuthType Basic**: This line specifies the authentication type
  that we are implementing. This type will implement password authentication using a password file.

- **AuthName**: This sets the message for the authentication dialog box. You should keep this generic so that unauthorized users won't gain any information about what is being protected.

- **AuthUserFile**: This sets the location of the password file that will be used for authentication. This should be outside of the directories that are being served. We will create this file shortly.

- **Require valid-user**: This specifies that only authenticated users should be given access to this resource. This is what actually stops unauthorized users from entering.

When you are finished, save and close the file.

Create the .htpasswd file for authentication
Now that we have specified a location for our password file through the use of the *AuthUserFiledirective* within our .htaccess file, we need to create this file. We actually need an additional package to complete this process:

sudo apt-get install apache2-utils

then, we will have the htpasswd utility available. The location that we selected for the password file was *"/etc/phpmyadmin/.htpasswd"*. Let's create this file and pass it an initial user by typing:

sudo htpasswd -c /etc/phpmyadmin/.htpasswd username

You will be prompted to select and confirm a password for the user you are creating. The file is created with the hashed password that

77

you entered. If you want to enter an additional user, you need to do that without the '-c' flag, like this:

sudo htpasswd /etc/phpmyadmin/.htpasswd additionaluser

Now, when you access your phpMyAdmin subdirectory, you will be prompted for the additional account name and password that you just configured:

http://domain_name_or_IP/phpmyadmin

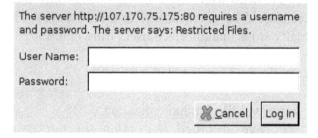

You should now have phpMyAdmin configured and ready to use on the server. Using this interface, you can easily create databases, users, tables, etc., and perform the usual operations like deleting and modifying structures and data, without access the command line at all to perform this kind of operations.

Web Analytics

There're a lot of good web analytics application, written not only in PHP that can be utilized to track the traffic passing about our websites. For instance *Piwik* is an open-source analytics system, and it provides a more personalized solution than the big global '*Google Analytics*' as it lets you have ownership and more control of the data, shows detailed traffic in real-time, and it has more stylistic graphs to see your data more effectively.

Installation
First, install some additional software that will be needed later on:

apt-get install unzip php5-gd

and restart Apache:

sudo service apache2 restart

go to the default root directory of Apache:

cd /var/www   or often
cd /var/www/html   depending of your settings;

download latest Piwik zip file:

wget http://builds.piwik.org/latest.zip

or recently also:

wget http://builds.piwik.org/piwik.zip

uncompress the zip file with the new tool lately installed:

unzip latest.zip   or   *unzip piwik.zip*

clean up the unneeded files:

*rm *html *zip*

Set the correct file permissions:

chown -R www-data:www-data /var/www/piwik

create a fresh database and a user for piwik; log in to MySQL server as *root*:

sudo mysql -u root –p

create the database "*db_piwik*", add new user "*piwik*" and add new password "*piwikpsw*" for this user:

mysql> CREATE DATABASE db_piwik CHARACTER SET='utf8';
mysql> CREATE USER 'piwik'@'localhost' IDENTIFIED BY 'piwikpsw';

mysql> GRANT ALL PRIVILEGES ON db_piwik. TO piwik@localhost WITH GRANT OPTION;*

mysql> FLUSH PRIVILEGES;
mysql> quit

the rest of the process will go through the GUI web installer throw the web browser:

http://domain_name_or_IP/piwik

when asked enter *127.0.01* or *localhost* as 'database server', then login and password as *piwik* and *piwikpsw,* table prefix *piwik_* the screen will show 'Tables created with sucess!' – complete the remaining information as site name, email address and what so ever to finish the installation.

Tip: often happens, installing some scripts, it's necessary to remove the installation(s) directories at the end of the installation process; to allow the server to do this automatically without know in advance which directory will needed to be removed, just set up the whole read/write permissions as follow:

sudo chmod –R 777 /var/www/html/install-path

then perform and finish the GUI installation, confirming the installation script to remove the desired directories to its liking; after this, go back to the terminal and set up again the correct read/write permissions:

sudo chmod –R 755 /var/www/html/install-path

sudo find /var/www/html/install-path/. -type f -exec chmod 644 {} ;

then set up eventually other different file and folder read/write permissions if required from the script, checking its manual or the online documentation.

In general this will help to perform any kind of script installation avoiding files & folders permissions inadequacies, but

Warning!
Always remember to chmod back
to 755 folders and to 644 files!

.. Example of installation of a more complex application

Introduction

We will proceed to the installation of a real time collaboration (RTC) server-based solutions, using a widely adopted open protocol for instant messaging, XMPP (also called Jabber).

Installation

If not already done, it's time to make the system up to date:

sudo apt-get update && sudo apt-get upgrade

install the latest version of Oracle JRE/JDK, use personal package archieve (PPA) WEBUPD8 to install it:

sudo apt-get install python-software-properties
sudo add-apt-repository ppa:webupd8team/java
sudo apt-get update

if you are using OpenJDK, remove it to minimise any Java conflicts:

*sudo apt-get remove --purge openjdk**

install Oracle Java 8 version:

sudo apt-get install oracle-java8-installer

create new MySQL database for Openfire; log in to MySQL Server as root:

sudo mysql -u root -p

create the database "dbopenfire", add new user "openfire" and add new password "openfirepwd" for user "openfire":

mysql> CREATE DATABASE dbopenfire CHARACTER SET='utf8';

mysql> CREATE USER 'openfire'@'localhost' IDENTIFIED BY 'openfirepwd';

mysql> GRANT ALL PRIVILEGES ON dbopenfire.* TO openfire@localhost WITH GRANT OPTION;

mysql> FLUSH PRIVILEGES;

mysql> quit

download and install *'openfire'*. At the time of this proceedings the latest release is v3.9.3 - download the deb. package of 'Openfire 3.9.3' from the 'Ignite Realtime' download page:

cd /tmp

wget download.igniterealtime.org/openfire/openfire_3.9.3_all.deb

install openfire_3.93_all.deb with dpkg command:

sudo dpkg -i openfire_3.9.3_all.deb

sudo apt-get install rpl
sudo rpl '6-sun' '8-oracle' /etc/init.d/openfire
sudo service openfire start

you need to setup firewall and allow some ports for openfire on the Linux server. Using ufw command:

sudo ufw allow 9090/tcp
sudo ufw allow 9091/tcp

sudo ufw allow 5222/tcp
sudo ufw allow 7777/tcp
sudo ufw allow 7443/tcp
sudo ufw allow 7070/tcp
sudo ufw allow 3478/tcp
sudo ufw allow 3479/tcp

or using iptables:

sudo iptables -A INPUT -p tcp -m tcp --dport 9090 -j ACCEPT
sudo iptables -A INPUT -p tcp -m tcp --dport 9091 -j ACCEPT
sudo iptables -A INPUT -p tcp -m tcp --dport 5222 -j ACCEPT
sudo iptables -A INPUT -p tcp -m tcp --dport 7777 -j ACCEPT
sudo iptables -A INPUT -p tcp -m tcp --dport 7443 -j ACCEPT
sudo iptables -A INPUT -p tcp -m tcp --dport 7070 -j ACCEPT
sudo iptables -A INPUT -p tcp -m tcp --dport 3478 -j ACCEPT
sudo iptables -A INPUT -p tcp -m tcp --dport 3479 -j ACCEPT

Now leave the command console. Next, we'll continue with con-figuration through a web browser. Reach the VPS server replacing "mydomain" with your FQDN or your public IP address, opening it with your favorite browser:

http://mydomain:9090/setup/index.jsp

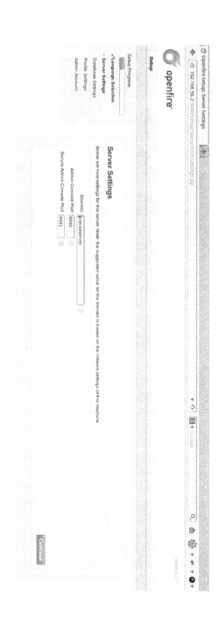

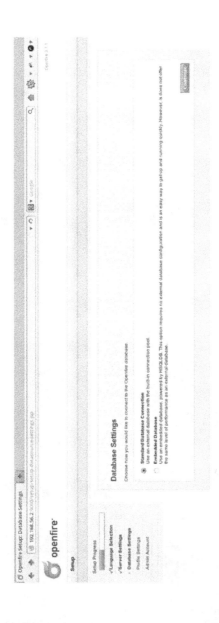

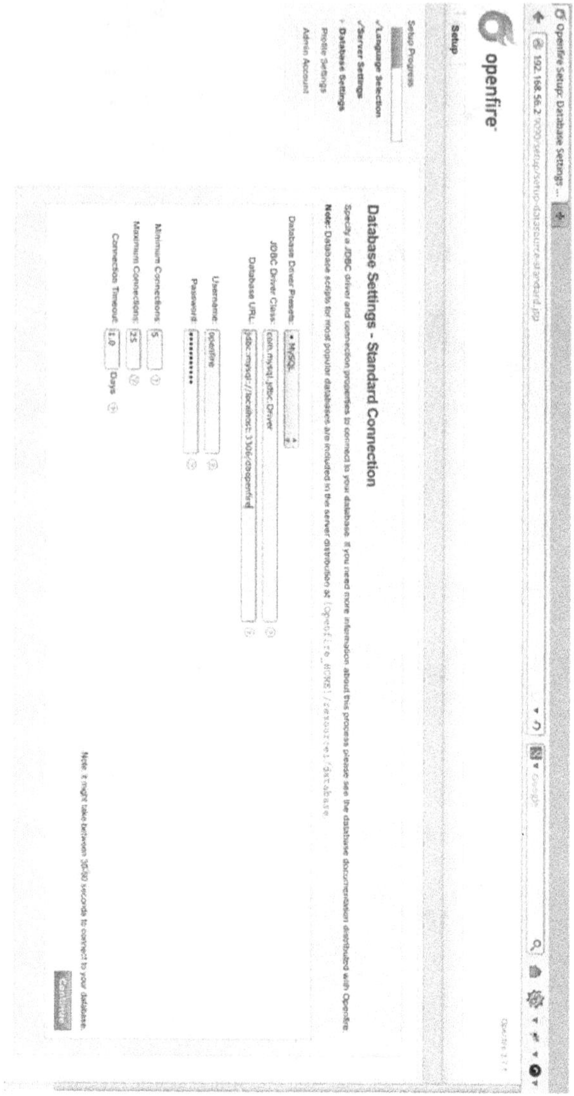
Openfire Setup: Database Settings ...
openfire
Setup
Setup Progress
Language Selection
Server Settings
Database Settings
Profile Settings
Admin Account
Database Settings - Standard Connection
Database Driver Presets:
MySQL
JDBC Driver Class:
com.mysql.jdbc.Driver
Database URL:
Username:
openfire
Password:
Minimum Connections:
5
Maximum Connections:
25
Connection Timeout:
1.0
Days
Continue

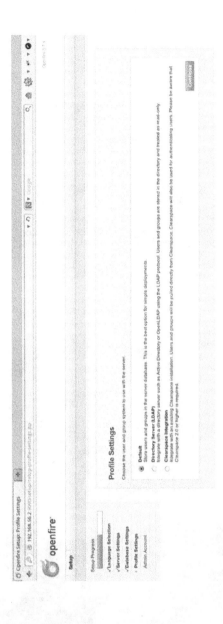

VPS TOOLKIT

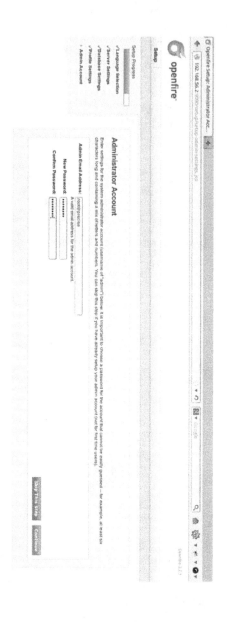

90

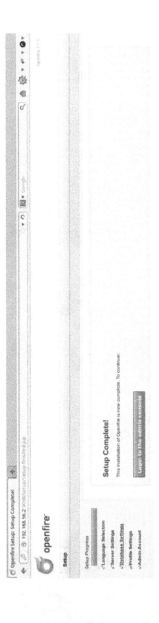

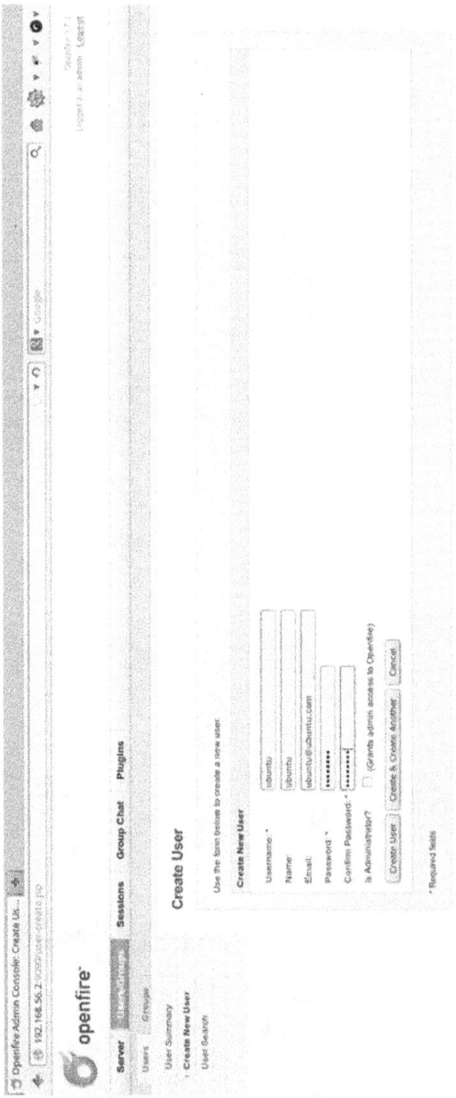
openfire
Server
Sessions
Group Chat
Plugins
Users
User Summary
Create New User
User Search
Create User
Use the form below to create a new user.
Create New User
Username: *
Name:
Email:
Password: *
Confirm Password: *
Is Administrator?
(Grants admin access to Openfire)
Create User
Create & Create Another
Cancel
* Required fields

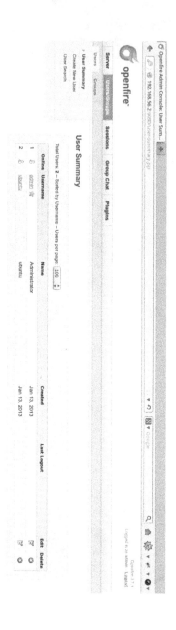

Instant Messaging Clients

You need to download and install an IM/VOIP client software on all PC/Laptop to connect with the Openfire Server. You can install any IM client that uses the XMPP/Jabber protocol for example the excellent Pidgin, it available for Linux Ubuntu, Windows, and Mac OSX. For Ubuntu users *pidgin* can be installed from the Ubuntu Software Center or by the Terminal:

sudo apt-get install pidgin

when done, make sure that you select *XMPP*.

The native cross plaform client for Openfire is *Spark*, it also available for *Linux*, *Windows* and *Mac OSX*. By the Terminal again, download spark from *IgniteRealTime* Download Page, and install it on Ubuntu desktop edition (the latest release when this was written, Ver. 2.6.3):

wget http://download.igniterealtime.org/spark/spark_2_6_3.tar.gz
tar -zxvf spark_2_6_3.tar.gz

sudo mkdir /opt/spark
sudo mv Spark/* /opt/spark/

Create a desktop launcher file - to the Terminal run the following command:

sudo nano /usr/share/applications/spark.desktop

[Desktop Entry]
Name=Spark
Version=2.6.3
GenericName=Spark

X-GNOME-FullName=Spark
Comment=ignite realtime Spark IM client
Type=Application
Categories=Application;Utility;
Path=/opt/spark
Exec=/bin/bash Spark
Terminal=false
StartupNotify=true
Icon=/opt/spark/logo-spark.png
TargetEnvironment=Unity
sudo cd /opt/spark

sudo wget https://dl.dropbox.com/u/50880014/spark.png

now, you'll finally be able to search for *Spark* in you unity dash and launch Spark:

Afterwords

We started with a fresh installation of a Virtual Private Server by the service-provider. Then, we've settled in the necessary components to the Linux Server to be up and running and then we deployed some web applications.

Webmaster who wants to take a step ahead toward operations from space-hosting to more complete and powerful server management, may use this cue in a schematic and safely way, increasing both the productivity and the performance side.

I hope this can help to take a step ahead to improve creativity.

VPS TOOLKIT

Bibliography – Resources & References

Operating Systems

Ubuntu official	www.ubuntu.com
Microsoft Windows	windows.microsoft.com
Apple OS X	www.apple.com/osx/

Applications

PuTTY	www.putty.org
TeamViewer	www.teamviewer.com
RealVNC	www.realvnc.com
Pidgin	www.pidgin.im

Web-Servers and Software

Comparison of Web Server Software	en.wikipedia.org
Apache Web Server	www.apache.org
OpenSSH	www.openssh.org
Bind9	www.isc.org
vsftpd FTP Server	vsftpd.beasts.org
MySQL database	www.mysql.com
phpMyadmin	www.phpmyadmin.net

Scripting Languages

PHP:
Hypertext Preprocessor   www.php.net

Other resources & references

www.digitalocean.com;

www.piwik.org;

www.filezilla-project.org;

www.cyberduck.io

Personal Notes

www.ingramcontent.com/pod-product-compliance
Lightning Source LLC
Chambersburg PA
CBHW071228050326
40689CB00011B/2491